CW00602020

First published by Ravette Publishing 2014

Ravette Publishing Limited
PO Box 876
Horsham
West Sussex RH12 9GH

ISBN: 978-1-84161-377-2

SCORPION POSE
VRISCHIKASANA

- Increases blood flow to the brain
- Revitalizes body systems
- Increases mind-body coordination
- Tones spinal nerves

Luna

CAT-COW POSE VARIATION
MARJARIASANA-BITILASANA

- Massages the spine and belly organs

- Stretches the neck and front torso

- Aligns the body

Jaya

SLEEPING VISHNU POSE
ANANTASANA

- Improves balance and blood circulation

- Stretches and tones the hamstrings and calves

- Helps relieve some forms of backache

Kai

TREE POSE
VRKSASANA

- Strengthens the thighs, calves, ankles, and spine

- Stretches the groin, chest and shoulders

- Improves sense of balance

LOTUS POSE
DHYANA

- Calms and focuses the mind

- Relaxes tension

- Centres the heart

LiLa

WARRIOR II
VIRABHADRASANA II

- Strengthens and stretches the legs and ankles

- Relieves backache

- Increases stamina

ZEBASTIAN

ONE-ARM HANDSTAND
EKA HASTA ADHO MUKHA VRKSASANA

- Improves balance

- Stretches the shoulders, arms
  and abdominal muscles

- Strengthens the arms and wrists

LiLLY

COBRA POSE
BHUJANGASANA

- Tones the back muscles

- Helps relieve and prevent lower backache

- Improves concentration

Kestrel

LORD OF THE DANCE POSE
NATARAJASANA

- Strengthens the legs and ankles
- Stretches the shoulders and chest
- Improves sense of balance

LiLa

WARRIOR III POSE
VIRABHADRASANA III

- Increases flexibility

- Strengthens the legs and abdomen

- Improves balance and core strength

Zane

HALF MOON POSE
ARDHA CHANDRASANA

- Strengthens the abdomen, ankles and spine

- Improves coordination and sense of balance

- Improves digestion

Vaughn

HEADSTAND
SIRSASANA

- Improves sense of balance

- Stretches the shoulders, arms and abdominal muscles

- Strengthens arms and wrists

- Increases blood flow to the brain